THIS BOOK
BELONGS TO

NAME

PHONE

MAIL

ADDRESS

NOTES

2019 CALENDAR

JANUARY 2019

Su	M	Tu	W	Th	F	Sa
30	31	1	2	3	4	5
6	7	8	9	10	11	12
13	14	15	16	17	18	19
20	21	22	23	24	25	26
27	28	29	30	31	1	2

FEBRUARY 2019

Su	M	Tu	W	Th	F	Sa
27	28	29	30	31	1	2
3	4	5	6	7	8	9
10	11	12	13	14	15	16
17	18	19	20	21	22	23
24	25	26	27	28	1	2

MARCH 2019

Su	M	Tu	W	Th	F	Sa
24	25	26	27	28	1	2
3	4	5	6	7	8	9
10	11	12	13	14	15	16
17	18	19	20	21	22	23
24	25	26	27	28	29	30
31	1	2	3	4	5	6

APRIL 2019

Su	M	Tu	W	Th	F	Sa
31	1	2	3	4	5	6
7	8	9	10	11	12	13
14	15	16	17	18	19	20
21	22	23	24	25	26	27
28	29	30	1	2	3	4

MAY 2019

Su	M	Tu	W	Th	F	Sa
28	29	30	1	2	3	4
5	6	7	8	9	10	11
12	13	14	15	16	17	18
19	20	21	22	23	24	25
26	27	28	29	30	31	1

JUNE 2019

Su	M	Tu	W	Th	F	Sa
26	27	28	29	30	31	1
2	3	4	5	6	7	8
9	10	11	12	13	14	15
16	17	18	19	20	21	22
23	24	25	26	27	28	29
30	1	2	3	4	5	6

JULY 2019

Su	M	Tu	W	Th	F	Sa
30	1	2	3	4	5	6
7	8	9	10	11	12	13
14	15	16	17	18	19	20
21	22	23	24	25	26	27
28	29	30	31	1	2	3

AUGUST 2019

Su	M	Tu	W	Th	F	Sa
28	29	30	31	1	2	3
4	5	6	7	8	9	10
11	12	13	14	15	16	17
18	19	20	21	22	23	24
25	26	27	28	29	30	31

SEPTEMBER 2019

Su	M	Tu	W	Th	F	Sa
1	2	3	4	5	6	7
8	9	10	11	12	13	14
15	16	17	18	19	20	21
22	23	24	25	26	27	28
29	30	1	2	3	4	5

OCTOBER 2019

Su	M	Tu	W	Th	F	Sa
29	30	1	2	3	4	5
6	7	8	9	10	11	12
13	14	15	16	17	18	19
20	21	22	23	24	25	26
27	28	29	30	31	1	2

NOVEMBER 2019

Su	M	Tu	W	Th	F	Sa
27	28	29	30	31	1	2
3	4	5	6	7	8	9
10	11	12	13	14	15	16
17	18	19	20	21	22	23
24	25	26	27	28	29	30

DECEMBER 2019

Su	M	Tu	W	Th	F	Sa
1	2	3	4	5	6	7
8	9	10	11	12	13	14
15	16	17	18	19	20	21
22	23	24	25	26	27	28
29	30	31	1	2	3	4

IMPORTANT DATES

IMPORTANT DATES

2019 **GOAL** SETTINGS

PERSONAL GOALS:

PROFESSIONAL GOALS:

FINANCIAL GOALS:

BOOKS TO READ:

PLACES TO GO:

I'M GRATEFUL FOR:

JANUARY 2019

Sun	Mon	Tues	Wed	Thu	Fri	Sat
30	31	1	2	3	4	5
6	7	8	9	10	11	12
13	14	15	16	17	18	19
20	21	22	23	24	25	26
27	28	29	30	31	1	2

NOTES:

JANUARY 2019

31 MONDAY ^{DECEMBER}

1 TUESDAY

2 WEDNESDAY

JANUARY 2019

3 THURSDAY

4 FRIDAY

5 SATURDAY

6 SUNDAY

JANUARY 2019

7 MONDAY

8 TUESDAY

9 WEDNESDAY

JANUARY 2019

10 THURSDAY

11 FRIDAY

12 SATURDAY

13 SUNDAY

JANUARY 2019

14 MONDAY

15 TUESDAY

16 WEDNESDAY

JANUARY 2019

17 THURSDAY

18 FRIDAY

19 SATURDAY

20 SUNDAY

JANUARY 2019

21 MONDAY

22 TUESDAY

23 WEDNESDAY

JANUARY 2019

24 THURSDAY

25 FRIDAY

26 SATURDAY

27 SUNDAY

JANUARY 2019

28 MONDAY

29 TUESDAY

30 WEDNESDAY

JANUARY 2019

31 THURSDAY

1 FRIDAY FEBRUARY

2 SATURDAY FEBRUARY

3 SUNDAY FEBRUARY

NOTES

FEBRUARY 2019

Sun	Mon	Tues	Wed	Thu	Fri	Sat
27	28	29	30	31	1	2
3	4	5	6	7	8	9
10	11	12	13	14	15	16
17	18	19	20	21	22	23
24	25	26	27	28	1	2

NOTES:

FEBRUARY 2019

31 THURSDAY JANUARY

1 FRIDAY

2 SATURDAY

3 SUNDAY

FEBRUARY 2019

4 MONDAY

5 TUESDAY

6 WEDNESDAY

FEBRUARY 2019

7 THURSDAY

8 FRIDAY

9 SATURDAY

10 SUNDAY

FEBRUARY 2019

11 MONDAY

12 TUESDAY

13 WEDNESDAY

FEBRUARY 2019

14 THURSDAY

15 FRIDAY

16 SATURDAY

17 SUNDAY

FEBRUARY 2019

18 MONDAY

19 TUESDAY

20 WEDNESDAY

FEBRUARY 2019

21 THURSDAY

22 FRIDAY

23 SATURDAY

24 SUNDAY

FEBRUARY 2019

25 MONDAY

26 TUESDAY

27 WEDNESDAY

FEBRUARY 2019

28 THURSDAY

1 FRIDAY MARCH

2 SATURDAY MARCH

3 SUNDAY MARCH

MARCH 2019

Sun	Mon	Tues	Wed	Thu	Fri	Sat
24	25	26	27	28	1	2
3	4	5	6	7	8	9
10	11	12	13	14	15	16
17	18	19	20	21	22	23
24	25	26	27	28	29	30
31	1	2	3	4	5	6

NOTES:

MARCH 2019

28 THURSDAY FEBRUARY

1 FRIDAY

2 SATURDAY

3 SUNDAY

MARCH 2019

4 MONDAY

5 TUESDAY

6 WEDNESDAY

MARCH 2019

7 THURSDAY

8 FRIDAY

9 SATURDAY

10 SUNDAY

MARCH 2019

11 MONDAY

12 TUESDAY

13 WEDNESDAY

MARCH 2019

14 THURSDAY

15 FRIDAY

16 SATURDAY

17 SUNDAY

MARCH 2019

18 MONDAY

19 TUESDAY

20 WEDNESDAY

MARCH 2019

21 THURSDAY

22 FRIDAY

23 SATURDAY

24 SUNDAY

MARCH 2019

25 MONDAY

26 TUESDAY

27 WEDNESDAY

MARCH 2019

28 THURSDAY

29 FRIDAY

30 SATURDAY

31 SUNDAY

APRIL 2019

Sun	Mon	Tues	Wed	Thu	Fri	Sat
31	1	2	3	4	5	6
7	8	9	10	11	12	13
14	15	16	17	18	19	20
21	22	23	24	25	26	27
28	29	30	1	2	3	4

NOTES:

APRIL 2019

1 MONDAY

2 TUESDAY

3 WEDNESDAY

APRIL 2019

4 THURSDAY

5 FRIDAY

6 SATURDAY

7 SUNDAY

APRIL 2019

8 MONDAY

9 TUESDAY

10 WEDNESDAY

APRIL 2019

11 THURSDAY

12 FRIDAY

13 SATURDAY

14 SUNDAY

APRIL 2019

15 MONDAY

16 TUESDAY

17 WEDNESDAY

APRIL 2019

18 THURSDAY

19 FRIDAY

20 SATURDAY

21 SUNDAY

APRIL 2019

22 MONDAY

23 TUESDAY

24 WEDNESDAY

APRIL 2019

25 THURSDAY

26 FRIDAY

27 SATURDAY

28 SUNDAY

APRIL 2019

29 MONDAY

30 TUESDAY

1 WEDNESDAY ^{MAY}

MAY 2019

Sun	Mon	Tues	Wed	Thu	Fri	Sat
28	29	30	1	2	3	4
5	6	7	8	9	10	11
12	13	14	15	16	17	18
19	20	21	22	23	24	25
26	27	28	29	30	31	1

NOTES:

MAY 2019

29 MONDAY ^{MARCH}

30 TUESDAY ^{MARCH}

1 WEDNESDAY

MAY 2019

2 THURSDAY

3 FRIDAY

4 SATURDAY

5 SUNDAY

MAY 2019

6 MONDAY

7 TUESDAY

8 WEDNESDAY

MAY 2019

9 THURSDAY

10 FRIDAY

11 SATURDAY

12 SUNDAY

MAY 2019

13 MONDAY

14 TUESDAY

15 WEDNESDAY

MAY 2019

16 THURSDAY

17 FRIDAY

18 SATURDAY

19 SUNDAY

MAY 2019

20 MONDAY

21 TUESDAY

22 WEDNESDAY

MAY 2019

23 THURSDAY

24 FRIDAY

25 SATURDAY

26 SUNDAY

MAY 2019

27 MONDAY

28 TUESDAY

29 WEDNESDAY

MAY 2019

30 THURSDAY

31 FRIDAY

1 SATURDAY JUNE

2 SUNDAY JUNE

NOTES

JUNE 2019

Sun	Mon	Tues	Wed	Thu	Fri	Sat
26	27	28	29	30	31	1
2	3	4	5	6	7	8
9	10	11	12	13	14	15
16	17	18	19	20	21	22
23	24	25	26	27	28	29
30	1	2	3	4	5	6

NOTES:

JUNE 2019

30 THURSDAY ^{MAY}

31 FRIDAY ^{MAY}

1 SATURDAY

2 SUNDAY

JUNE 2019

3 MONDAY

4 TUESDAY

5 WEDNESDAY

JUNE 2019

6 THURSDAY

7 FRIDAY

8 SATURDAY

9 SUNDAY

JUNE 2019

10 MONDAY

11 TUESDAY

12 WEDNESDAY

JUNE 2019

13 THURSDAY

14 FRIDAY

15 SATURDAY

16 SUNDAY

JUNE 2019

17 MONDAY

18 TUESDAY

19 WEDNESDAY

JUNE 2019

20 THURSDAY

21 FRIDAY

22 SATURDAY

23 SUNDAY

JUNE 2019

24 MONDAY

25 TUESDAY

26 WEDNESDAY

JUNE 2019

27 THURSDAY

28 FRIDAY

29 SATURDAY

30 SUNDAY

JULY 2019

Sun	Mon	Tues	Wed	Thu	Fri	Sat
30	1	2	3	4	5	6
7	8	9	10	11	12	13
14	15	16	17	18	19	20
21	22	23	24	25	26	27
28	29	30	31	1	2	3

NOTES:

JULY 2019

1 MONDAY

2 TUESDAY

3 WEDNESDAY

JULY 2019

4 THURSDAY

5 FRIDAY

6 SATURDAY

7 SUNDAY

JULY 2019

8 MONDAY

9 TUESDAY

10 WEDNESDAY

JULY 2019

11 THURSDAY

12 FRIDAY

13 SATURDAY

14 SUNDAY

JULY 2019

15 MONDAY

16 TUESDAY

17 WEDNESDAY

JULY 2019

18 THURSDAY

19 FRIDAY

20 SATURDAY

21 SUNDAY

JULY 2019

22 MONDAY

23 TUESDAY

24 WEDNESDAY

JULY 2019

25 THURSDAY

26 FRIDAY

27 SATURDAY

28 SUNDAY

JULY 2019

29 MONDAY

30 TUESDAY

31 WEDNESDAY

AUGUST 2019

Sun	Mon	Tues	Wed	Thu	Fri	Sat
28	29	30	31	1	2	3
4	5	6	7	8	9	10
11	12	13	14	15	16	17
18	19	20	21	22	23	24
25	26	27	28	29	30	31

NOTES:

AUGUST 2019

1 THURSDAY

2 FRIDAY

3 SATURDAY

4 SUNDAY

AUGUST 2019

5 MONDAY

6 TUESDAY

7 WEDNESDAY

AUGUST 2019

8 THURSDAY

9 FRIDAY

10 SATURDAY

11 SUNDAY

AUGUST 2019

12 MONDAY

13 TUESDAY

14 WEDNESDAY

AUGUST 2019

15 THURSDAY

16 FRIDAY

17 SATURDAY

18 SUNDAY

AUGUST 2019

19 MONDAY

20 TUESDAY

21 WEDNESDAY

AUGUST 2019

22 THURSDAY

23 FRIDAY

24 SATURDAY

25 SUNDAY

AUGUST 2019

26 MONDAY

27 TUESDAY

28 WEDNESDAY

AUGUST 2019

29 THURSDAY

30 FRIDAY

31 SATURDAY

1 SUNDAY SEPTEMBER

SEPTEMBER 2019

Sun	Mon	Tues	Wed	Thu	Fri	Sat
1	2	3	4	5	6	7
8	9	10	11	12	13	14
15	16	17	18	19	20	21
22	23	24	25	26	27	28
29	30	1	2	3	4	5

NOTES:

SEPTEMBER 2019

29 THURSDAY AUGUST

30 FRIDAY AUGUST

31 SATURDAY AUGUST

1 SUNDAY

SEPTEMBER 2019

2 MONDAY

3 TUESDAY

4 WEDNESDAY

SEPTEMBER 2019

5 THURSDAY

6 FRIDAY

7 SATURDAY

8 SUNDAY

SEPTEMBER 2019

9 MONDAY

10 TUESDAY

11 WEDNESDAY

SEPTEMBER 2019

12 THURSDAY

13 FRIDAY

14 SATURDAY

15 SUNDAY

SEPTEMBER 2019

16 MONDAY

17 TUESDAY

18 WEDNESDAY

SEPTEMBER 2019

19 THURSDAY

20 FRIDAY

21 SATURDAY

22 SUNDAY

SEPTEMBER 2019

23 MONDAY

24 TUESDAY

25 WEDNESDAY

SEPTEMBER 2019

26 THURSDAY

27 FRIDAY

28 SATURDAY

29 SUNDAY

SEPTEMBER 2019

30 MONDAY

1 TUESDAY OCTOBER

2 WEDNESDAY OCTOBER

NOTES

OCTOBER 2019

Sun	Mon	Tues	Wed	Thu	Fri	Sat
29	30	1	2	3	4	5
6	7	8	9	10	11	12
13	14	15	16	17	18	19
20	21	22	23	24	25	26
27	28	29	30	31	1	2

NOTES:

OCTOBER 2019

30 MONDAY SEPTEMBER

1 TUESDAY

2 WEDNESDAY

OCTOBER 2019

3 THURSDAY

4 FRIDAY

5 SATURDAY

6 SUNDAY

OCTOBER 2019

7 MONDAY

8 TUESDAY

9 WEDNESDAY

OCTOBER 2019

10 THURSDAY

11 FRIDAY

12 SATURDAY

13 SUNDAY

OCTOBER 2019

14 MONDAY

15 TUESDAY

16 WEDNESDAY

OCTOBER 2019

17 THURSDAY

18 FRIDAY

19 SATURDAY

20 SUNDAY

OCTOBER 2019

21 MONDAY

22 TUESDAY

23 WEDNESDAY

OCTOBER 2019

24 THURSDAY

25 FRIDAY

26 SATURDAY

27 SUNDAY

OCTOBER 2019

28 MONDAY

29 TUESDAY

30 WEDNESDAY

OCTOBER 2019

31 THURSDAY

1 FRIDAY NOVEMBER

2 SATURDAY NOVEMBER

3 SUNDAY NOVEMBER

NOTES

NOVEMBER 2019

Sun	Mon	Tues	Wed	Thu	Fri	Sat
27	28	29	30	31	1	2
3	4	5	6	7	8	9
10	11	12	13	14	15	16
17	18	19	20	21	22	23
24	25	26	27	28	29	30

NOTES:

NOVEMBER 2019

31 THURSDAY OCTOBER

1 FRIDAY

2 SATURDAY

3 SUNDAY

NOVEMBER 2019

4 MONDAY

5 TUESDAY

6 WEDNESDAY

NOVEMBER 2019

7 THURSDAY

8 FRIDAY

9 SATURDAY

10 SUNDAY

NOVEMBER 2019

11 MONDAY

12 TUESDAY

13 WEDNESDAY

NOVEMBER 2019

14 THURSDAY

15 FRIDAY

16 SATURDAY

17 SUNDAY

NOVEMBER 2019

18 MONDAY

19 TUESDAY

20 WEDNESDAY

NOVEMBER 2019

21 THURSDAY

22 FRIDAY

23 SATURDAY

24 SUNDAY

NOVEMBER 2019

25 MONDAY

26 TUESDAY

27 WEDNESDAY

NOVEMBER 2019

28 THURSDAY

29 FRIDAY

30 SATURDAY

1 SUNDAY DECEMBER

DECEMBER 2019

Sun	Mon	Tues	Wed	Thu	Fri	Sat
1	2	3	4	5	6	7
8	9	10	11	12	13	14
15	16	17	18	19	20	21
22	23	24	25	26	27	28
29	30	31	1	2	3	4

NOTES:

DECEMBER 2019

28 THURSDAY NOVEMBER

29 FRIDAY NOVEMBER

30 SATURDAY NOVEMBER

1 SUNDAY

DECEMBER 2019

2 MONDAY

3 TUESDAY

4 WEDNESDAY

DECEMBER 2019

5 THURSDAY

6 FRIDAY

7 SATURDAY

8 SUNDAY

DECEMBER 2019

9 MONDAY

10 TUESDAY

11 WEDNESDAY

DECEMBER 2019

12 THURSDAY

13 FRIDAY

14 SATURDAY

15 SUNDAY

DECEMBER 2019

16 MONDAY

17 TUESDAY

18 WEDNESDAY

DECEMBER 2019

19 THURSDAY

20 FRIDAY

21 SATURDAY

22 SUNDAY

DECEMBER 2019

23 MONDAY

24 TUESDAY

25 WEDNESDAY

DECEMBER 2019

26 THURSDAY

27 FRIDAY

28 SATURDAY

29 SUNDAY

DECEMBER 2019

30 MONDAY

31 TUESDAY

1 WEDNESDAY JANUARY 2020

END OF THE YEAR NOTES

CONTACTS

NAME	NAME
PHONE	PHONE
MAIL	MAIL
ADDRESS	ADDRESS
NOTES	NOTES
NAME	NAME
PHONE	PHONE
MAIL	MAIL
ADDRESS	ADDRESS
NOTES	NOTES
NAME	NAME
PHONE	PHONE
MAIL	MAIL
ADDRESS	ADDRESS
NOTES	NOTES
NAME	NAME
PHONE	PHONE
MAIL	MAIL
ADDRESS	ADDRESS
NOTES	NOTES
NAME	NAME
PHONE	PHONE
MAIL	MAIL
ADDRESS	ADDRESS
NOTES	NOTES

CONTACTS

NAME	NAME
PHONE	PHONE
MAIL	MAIL
ADDRESS	ADDRESS
NOTES	NOTES
NAME	NAME
PHONE	PHONE
MAIL	MAIL
ADDRESS	ADDRESS
NOTES	NOTES
NAME	NAME
PHONE	PHONE
MAIL	MAIL
ADDRESS	ADDRESS
NOTES	NOTES
NAME	NAME
PHONE	PHONE
MAIL	MAIL
ADDRESS	ADDRESS
NOTES	NOTES
NAME	NAME
PHONE	PHONE
MAIL	MAIL
ADDRESS	ADDRESS
NOTES	NOTES

CONTACTS

NAME

PHONE

MAIL

ADDRESS

NOTES

NAME

PHONE

MAIL

ADDRESS

NOTES

NAME

PHONE

MAIL

ADDRESS

NOTES

NAME

PHONE

MAIL

ADDRESS

NOTES

NAME

PHONE

MAIL

ADDRESS

NOTES

NAME

PHONE

MAIL

ADDRESS

NOTES

NAME

PHONE

MAIL

ADDRESS

NOTES

NAME

PHONE

MAIL

ADDRESS

NOTES

NAME

PHONE

MAIL

ADDRESS

NOTES

NAME

PHONE

MAIL

ADDRESS

NOTES

CONTACTS

NAME

PHONE

MAIL

ADDRESS

NOTES

NAME

PHONE

MAIL

ADDRESS

NOTES

NAME

PHONE

MAIL

ADDRESS

NOTES

NAME

PHONE

MAIL

ADDRESS

NOTES

NAME

PHONE

MAIL

ADDRESS

NOTES

NAME

PHONE

MAIL

ADDRESS

NOTES

NAME

PHONE

MAIL

ADDRESS

NOTES

NAME

PHONE

MAIL

ADDRESS

NOTES

NAME

PHONE

MAIL

ADDRESS

NOTES

NAME

PHONE

MAIL

ADDRESS

NOTES

PASSWORDS

NOTES

NOTES

NOTES

NOTES

NOTES

NOTES

NOTES

NOTES

NOTES

NOTES

NOTES

NOTES

Printed in Germany
by Amazon Distribution
GmbH, Leipzig